Next Generation ENERGY

ENERGY FROM NUCLEAR FISSION

Splitting the Atom

Nancy Dickmann

CRABTREE Publishing Company
www.crabtreebooks.com

Crabtree Publishing Company

www.crabtreebooks.com

Author: Nancy Dickmann

Editors: Sarah Eason, Jen Sanderson, and Shirley Duke

Proofreader: Katie Dicker and Wendy Scavuzzo

Editorial director: Kathy Middleton

Design: Paul Myerscough and Geoff Ward

Cover design: Paul Myerscough

Photo research: Sarah Eason and Jen Sanderson

Prepress technician: Margaret Amy Salter

Print coordinator: Margaret Amy Salter

Consultant: Richard Spilsbury, degree in Zoology, 30 years as an author and editor of educational science books

Written and produced for Crabtree Publishing by Calcium Creative

Photo Credits:

t=Top, bl=Bottom Left, br=Bottom Right

Dreamstime: Maura Reap pp. 19–20; Scott Prokop: p. 28; Thomas Jenkins p. 15; NASA: NASA/SDO: p. 26; Shutterstock: Alexander Kuguchin: p. 22; Andrea Danti: p. 21; Axily: p. 24; Chungking: pp. 6–7, 30–31; Curraheeshutter: p. 7; Denton Rumsey: p. 16; Designua: p. 12; Dotshock: pp. 3, 24–25; Everett Historical: pp. 8–9, 32; F. Enot: pp. 20–21; Ifong: p. 6; John Carnemolla: p. 11; Julius Fekete pp. 12–13; Kasezo: pp. 1, 26; Marcel Clemens: p. 17; Marcin Balcerzak: pp. 22–23; Martin Nemec: p. 25; Monkey Business Images: p. 28; Oliver Sved: pp. 14–15; Peter Hermes Furian: p. 8; Peter Sobolev: pp. 3, 10; QiuJu: Song p. 13; R. Classen: pp. 10–11; Radiokafka: p. 23; Sergey Kamshylin: pp. 18–19; Twin Design: pp. 26–27; ValeStock: pp. 4–5; View Apart: p. 5; Zhu Difeng: pp. 16–17, 28–29; Wikimedia Commons: Jason Paris: p. 14; Mike Garrett: p. 27; Z22: p. 18.

Cover: Shutterstock: Kasezo.

Library and Archives Canada Cataloguing in Publication

Dickmann, Nancy, author
    Energy from nuclear fission : splitting the atom / Nancy Dickmann.

(Next generation energy)
Includes index.
Issued in print and electronic formats.
ISBN 978-0-7787-1981-6 (bound).--
ISBN 978-0-7787-2004-1 (paperback).--
ISBN 978-1-4271-1639-0 (pdf).--
ISBN 978-1-4271-1631-4 (html)

    1. Nuclear energy--Juvenile literature. 2. Clean energy-- Juvenile literature. I. Title.

TK9148.D53 2015   j333.792'4   C2015-903218-0
                                          C2015-903219-9

Library of Congress Cataloging-in-Publication Data

Dickmann, Nancy, author.
 Energy from nuclear fission : splitting the atom / Nancy Dickmann.
    pages cm. -- (Next generation energy)
 Includes index.
 ISBN 978-0-7787-1981-6 (reinforced library binding : alk. paper) --
ISBN 978-0-7787-2004-1 (pbk. : alk. paper) --
ISBN 978-1-4271-1639-0 (electronic pdf : alk. paper) --
ISBN 978-1-4271-1631-4 (electronic html : alk. paper)
1. Nuclear energy--Juvenile literature. 2. Nuclear industry-- Juvenile literature. 3. Power resources--Juvenile literature. I. Title.

 QC792.5.D53 2016
 333.792'4--dc23

                  2015022002

Crabtree Publishing Company

www.crabtreebooks.com   1-800-387-7650

Printed in Canada/082015/BF20150630

Published in Canada
Crabtree Publishing
616 Welland Ave.
St. Catharines, Ontario
L2M 5V6

Published in the United States
Crabtree Publishing
PMB 59051
350 Fifth Avenue, 59th Floor
New York, New York 10118

Published in the United Kingdom
Crabtree Publishing
Maritime House
Basin Road North, Hove
BN41 1WR

Published in Australia
Crabtree Publishing
3 Charles Street
Coburg North
VIC, 3058

Contents

What Is Energy?

Everywhere you look, you can see energy being used. Energy is the ability to do work. It comes in many different forms. The food you eat provides chemical energy for your body to use. When you switch on a battery-powered appliance, the chemical energy changes to electrical energy. When you cook food on the stove, you are transferring heat energy from the burning gas to the ingredients.

We Need Energy

Our demand for energy is huge. We use it to fuel our automobiles, trains, and airplanes, to heat and light our homes, and power factories. We use energy from a variety of sources, from oil and natural gas to solar, wind, and hydroelectric power. Some of these energy sources, such as solar energy, are renewable. This means that they are based on resources such as sunlight and wind, which will never run out. Others, such as natural gas and oil, will eventually run out—they are nonrenewable. It takes millions of years for these fuels to form deep underground. Once we have used up what is there, we will need to find other sources of energy.

This pie chart shows how much of the world's electricity is generated using different types of power.

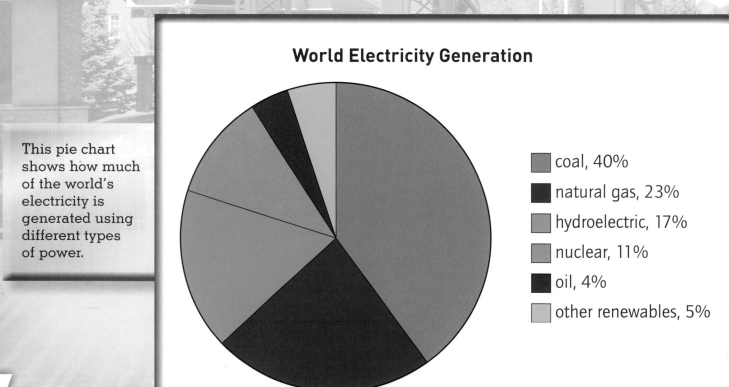

World Electricity Generation

- coal, 40%
- natural gas, 23%
- hydroelectric, 17%
- nuclear, 11%
- oil, 4%
- other renewables, 5%

No single type of energy source is perfect. Some sources such as coal and oil create **pollution**. Pollution is something introduced into the **environment** that causes harmful or poisonous effects.

Other energy sources can be unreliable or less effective. Some are more expensive to produce, and others—such as geothermal or solar energy— can be produced only in particular places where the conditions are right. Some energy sources are better for particular uses than others. For example, natural gas is a good way to produce electricity, but it is not practical for fueling cars. When choosing the type of energy to use, we need to balance all of these issues.

The bright lights of a busy city such as Las Vegas use a huge amount of electrical energy.

REWIND

People's need for vast amounts of energy is fairly recent. Just 150 years ago, electricity was not used to power lights and appliances. There were also no cars to use gasoline. Fuels such as wood, coal, and whale oil were burned for heat and light. In the time since electricity became widely available in homes, around the 1930s, engineers have invented countless appliances that use it. What do you think daily life might have been like before the 1930s?

Why Use Nuclear Energy?

The world's population is growing and the demand for energy is growing, too. More and more people are now able to afford automobiles, cell phones, air travel, and many other things that use energy. This means that the energy industry is under pressure to produce even more energy to meet the world's growing needs.

In the past, we relied heavily on **fossil fuels** such as coal, oil, and natural gas. These fuels are all formed from the decaying remains of living things that were buried under layers of deposits. This process takes millions of years. For many years, coal was burned to heat homes, as well as to provide electricity. Oil is turned into gasoline, aviation fuel, and other products that people rely on. However, these fuels have two big drawbacks. One is that people are using so much of them that supplies will soon run out. The other is that burning these fuels creates pollution in the form of **greenhouse gases** that contribute to **climate change**.

Flying is a quick way to travel, but it uses a lot of fuel. About 8 percent of the gasoline used in the United States is used to fuel airplanes.

Looking for Answers

Experts agree that an alternative to fossil fuels must be found. Renewable energy sources such as solar and wind power are becoming more available, but they are not yet ready to replace fossil fuels. They will probably never be able to replace them entirely. Recent innovations have meant that nuclear power is safer and cleaner than ever before. Could nuclear energy be the answer?

Scientists have known how to harness the energy of **nuclear reactions** for more than 70 years. The process is efficient, meaning that it supplies a large amount of energy using a small amount of fuel. It cannot yet be used to fuel cars, but it is already used to run electrical power stations. Could an increased use of nuclear power solve the world's energy problems?

Burning off excess gases helps reduce possible problems, but extracting fossil fuels is expensive. When accidents occur, they can damage the environment.

FAST FORWARD

One hundred years ago, no one knew how to generate electricity from solar, nuclear, or wind power. But now these technologies are more widely used. Energy use might look completely different in another 100 years, when fossil fuels will be nearly gone. What changes do you think will have to be made to the way we use energy? Explain your thinking.

Splitting the Atom

Everything in the universe, from tiny grains of sand and gigantic stars to living organisms, is made up of building blocks called **atoms**. Atoms are far too small to see, but they are made up of even smaller particles. At the center of an atom is the **nucleus**, which is a clump of particles called **protons** and **neutrons**. Around them is a field where even smaller particles called **electrons** exist.

The atoms of some substances such as **uranium** have nuclei that are unstable. Scientists discovered that firing a neutron at one of these atoms could make it split in two. This process is called **nuclear fission**. When the atom splits, it releases energy and it also releases neutrons. These neutrons then crash into other uranium atoms and cause them to split, too. As more and more atoms are split and release neutrons, it causes a chain reaction, releasing huge amounts of energy.

This diagram shows the start of a nuclear fission chain reaction.

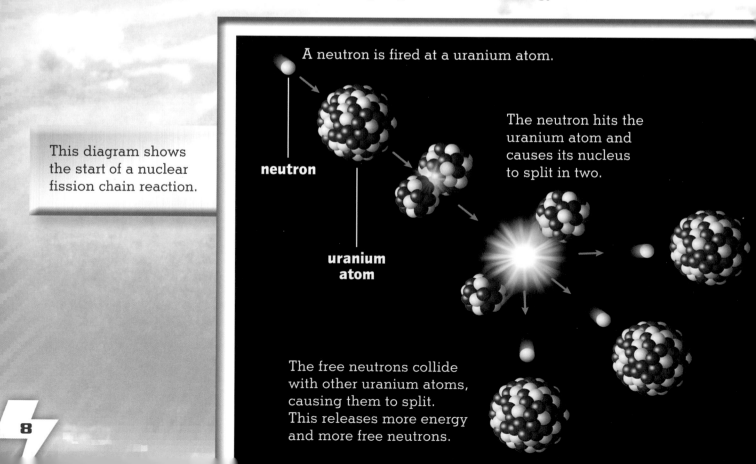

A neutron is fired at a uranium atom.

The neutron hits the uranium atom and causes its nucleus to split in two.

neutron

uranium atom

The free neutrons collide with other uranium atoms, causing them to split. This releases more energy and more free neutrons.

Figuring Out Fission

In the early 1900s, scientists first had the idea that a uranium nucleus might break up if it were bombarded with neutrons. In 1905, the German-born scientist Albert Einstein published the famous equation $E=mc^2$. This equation is a way of showing how much energy is contained in matter. In the 1930s, the Austrian physicist Lise Meitner and her nephew, Otto Frisch, proposed the theory that explained how this energy might be released. Building on their ideas, Otto Hahn and Fritz Strassmann successfully split a uranium atom in their Berlin laboratory in 1938, while Lise Meitner worked in Sweden after fleeing the Nazis. In 1942, Enrico Fermi and his team in the United States produced the first chain reaction.

Otto Hahn was awarded the Nobel Prize for his work on nuclear fission. Lise Meitner, one of of his two lab partners, was overlooked. The element meitnerium was later named after her.

REWIND

Scientists working on nuclear fission knew that it could be a useful energy source. However, after World War II broke out in 1939, scientists on both sides of the conflict worked on finding a way to use nuclear fission to make weapons. These nuclear bombs were used for the first time in 1945. Although the scientists knew that nuclear weapons were crucial for winning the war, many felt uncomfortable about inventing something so destructive. What choice would you have made in their place? Explain your thinking.

Nuclear Fuel

The main fuel used in nuclear fission is a type of uranium called uranium 235, or U-235. Like many other elements, uranium comes in different forms, or isotopes. Different isotopes of an element have the same number of protons, but a different number of neutrons. Each uranium atom has 92 protons, but its different isotopes have different numbers of neutrons. For example, U-235 has 143 neutrons, and gets its name because 92 + 143 = 235.

The most common form of uranium found in nature is U-238, which has 146 neutrons. Those three extra neutrons make a surprisingly big difference. U-238 is much more stable, and it does not split as easily as U-235. Unfortunately, although uranium is a fairly common element, U-235 is rare. Only about 0.7 percent of the uranium in Earth's crust is U-235. Most of the rest is U-238.

These fuel rods are ready to be used in a nuclear power station.

Making the Fuel

The main producers of uranium are Australia, Canada, Kazakhstan, and Russia. The uranium ore is dug up in enormous mines, then processed to separate the uranium from the other materials. The uranium ore contains a **radioactive** element called radium, which is not useful for nuclear fuel. Acid is used to remove the radium.

Finally, for the uranium to be useful as nuclear fuel, it must be purified, or **enriched**. This means increasing the proportion of U-235 in the mix from less than 1 percent up to 3 percent or more. However, some types of **reactors** can use fuel that is less enriched. Once the uranium is enriched, it is heated and formed into pellets about 1 inch (2.5 cm) long and 0.5 inch (1.3 cm) in diameter. These pellets are packed into long steel tubes called rods and collected together into bundles.

Uranium is often mined in open-pit mines, where the raw ore is scraped out of huge holes in the ground.

FAST FORWARD

Some scientists estimate that there is enough uranium on Earth to last for less than 100 years, if we keep using it at the same rate we are now. Eventually, we will need to find new ways of fueling nuclear power stations, but scientists are already working on this. What might happen when supplies of uranium run out, if we are unable to find alternatives?

Inside a Reactor

Nuclear fuel is most often used to generate electricity. Deep inside the reactor, nuclear fission takes place in the fuel rods and makes them heat up. The fuel rods are submerged in a coolant, which is usually water. The coolant's job is to keep the fuel rods from overheating.

To be safe, the nuclear reaction has to be kept under strict control. If too many nuclei split in a short amount of time, the huge amount of energy released could cause the reactor to explode. Control rods made of other substances help adjust the speed of the nuclear reaction. They absorb neutrons and they can be raised or lowered to speed up or slow down the fission process. Another possible problem is the neutrons moving too quickly. If they move too fast, they cannot split the other nuclei and the chain reaction stops. In many reactors, the coolant also helps by acting as a **moderator** to slow down the neutrons.

The next stage in the process is to convert the heat energy produced by the fuel rods into electrical energy. In most nuclear reactors, the fuel rods heat the coolant to temperatures of around 600° Fahrenheit (316°C).

This diagram shows how a nuclear reactor works. In a nuclear power station, the hot coolant is transported to a steam **generator**, where it produces steam to spin the **turbines**.

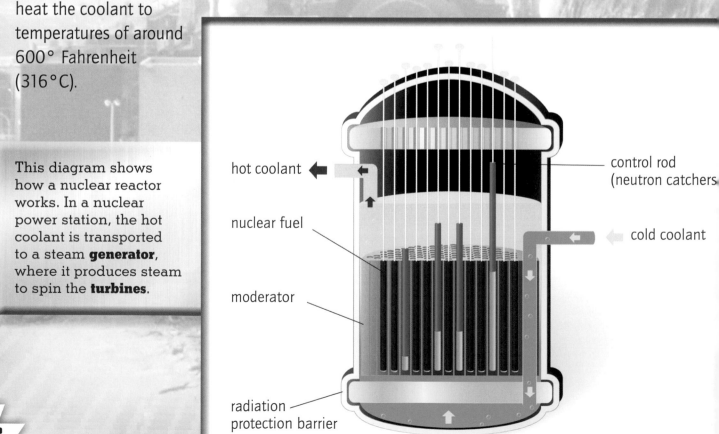

hot coolant

nuclear fuel

moderator

radiation protection barrier

control rod (neutron catchers)

cold coolant

However, the coolant is kept under **pressure** so that it cannot boil. Instead, the super-hot coolant is piped to a steam generator, where it heats clean water and turns it into steam.

Same but Different

The last stage of the electricity-generating process is the same as that used in a coal-fired or gas-fired power station. The steam spins a turbine, which is connected to a generator. The spinning of the turbine allows the generator to produce electricity. The steam is then cooled in a cooling tower. When it turns back into water, it can be used again in the steam generator.

Turbines are used in most types of electricity generation, from wind and wave to nuclear and coal-fired.

REWIND

Shippingport in Pennsylvania was one of the world's first nuclear power stations when it opened in 1957. It could produce about 100 **megawatts (MW)** of electricity. A megawatt is a measure for energy. There are 1 million watts in a megawatt. Thanks to improved technology, today's reactors are cheaper to build and more efficient. New designs also mean that they are safer. What effect do you think this has had on public acceptance of nuclear power?

Types of Reactors

Although the process of nuclear fission is the same, there are several different types of nuclear reactors in use today. The most common type is the pressurized water reactor (PWR), which uses heated coolant to make steam. There are more than 400 reactors in use around the world and about two thirds of these are PWRs.

In a PWR, the coolant water and the water heated for steam are kept completely separate. A boiling water reactor (BWR) is similar, but in these reactors, the water used as the coolant is also boiled to create steam. Together, these two types of reactors account for 88 percent of the world's nuclear reactors.

Another type is the pressurized heavy water reactor (PHWR). This reactor uses a substance called "heavy water"—an isotope of the hydrogen part of a water molecule—as a moderator, and sometimes as the coolant. Advanced gas-cooled reactors (AGRs) are common in the United Kingdom. They use carbon dioxide gas as a coolant and graphite as a moderator.

A Candu reactor is a type of pressurized heavy water reactor that is widely used in Canada.

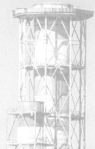

The Dungeness B nuclear power station in the United Kingdom uses an advanced gas-cooled reactor, or AGR.

Both of these types of reactors have the advantage of being able to use fuel that is less enriched than the fuel needed for PWRs or BWRs.

Endless Fuel?

One interesting type of reactor is the breeder reactor. These actually create more fuel than they use up, by converting the U-238 in their fuel rods to other substances that can be used as nuclear fuels. Some other reactors are designed to use thorium as a fuel. Thorium cannot be used on its own—it must be combined with another material, such as recycled plutonium. However, thorium is more abundant than uranium, it can be used to make other types of nuclear fuel, and it produces less nuclear waste. Nuclear waste is the material that nuclear fuel becomes after it is used in a reactor. It is radioactive, so it gives off harmful radiation.

REWIND

The RBMK reactor was a type often used in the former Soviet Union, starting in the 1950s. They could use unenriched uranium, which made them an attractive choice. However, they also had serious safety flaws. Some RBMK reactors are still in use in Russia, although they have been fitted with safety upgrades. Do you think efficiency or safety should be the most important factor when deciding which type of reactor to use?

How "Green" Is Nuclear Energy?

In the past few decades, we have learned more about the effects of the different types of energy that we use. Many of the most common fuels, such as oil and coal, pollute the environment and release harmful greenhouse gases such as carbon dioxide. We now know that it is important to use green energy, which causes less damage to the environment.

No fuel is completely green. For example, building wind turbines uses up fuel and resources. The turbines also make the countryside less attractive and they can affect birds and marine life when they are built in the oceans. But wind power is still greener than fuels such as coal; wind turbines do not emit, or give off, carbon dioxide; and wind power will never run out.

Is Nuclear Power Clean?

A nuclear power station releases only about 1 percent of the carbon dioxide that a coal-fired power station does. This is good news for global climate change, but it is only part of the picture. Mining the uranium and building the power stations uses fossil fuels and damages the environment.

The clouds coming out of a nuclear cooling tower are actually just harmless steam, not pollution.

However, the main problem with nuclear power is the radioactive waste produced by nuclear power stations. Nuclear waste stays radioactive for thousands of years, so it cannot just be thrown away or left where it is. Most nuclear waste is buried. The higher the level of radioactivity, the deeper it is placed underground. All nuclear waste remains dangerous, however.

Nuclear power uses up uranium. Like coal, oil, and natural gas, Earth has a limited supply of uranium, so this type of power is nonrenewable. Some types of breeder reactors create more fuel than they use, so they could be called renewable. These reactors are very rare, though.

It takes a lot of energy and dangerous chemicals to turn a lump of uranium ore into nuclear fuel.

The Energy Future: You Choose

Nuclear power produces virtually no greenhouse gases, but it does create hazardous waste. Based on what you have learned, do you think that nuclear power can be considered green? What do you think is the most important factor in deciding whether a type of energy is clean? Support your answers with examples from this book.

Dangers and Disasters

Another problem with nuclear energy is the risk of accidents. Of course, accidents can happen at any type of power station and most nuclear power stations are extremely safe. However, accidents at nuclear power stations can be more serious because of the dangerous radioactive substances used there. Exposure to **radiation** can cause cancer and extreme exposure is fatal.

Serious Accidents

At the Three Mile Island nuclear plant in Pennsylvania, an accident in 1979 nearly caused a **meltdown**. Meltdowns occur when the hot fuel burns its way through the bottom of a reactor. Although no one was hurt, it made many people nervous about the safety of nuclear power. A Hollywood movie about a fictional nuclear disaster had opened just a few weeks earlier, so the real accident got a lot of attention.

In 1986, there was an enormous explosion at the Chernobyl power station in what is now Ukraine.

NUCLEAR ACCIDENT AT THREE MILE ISLAND

On March 28, 1979, and for several days thereafter .. as a result of technical malfunctions and human error .. Three Mile Island's Unit 2 Nuclear Generating Station was the scene of the nation's worst commercial nuclear accident. Radiation was released, a part of the nuclear core was damaged, and thousands of residents evacuated the area. Events here would cause basic changes throughout the world's nuclear power industry.

PENNSYLVANIA HISTORICAL AND MUSEUM COMMISSION   1999

The Three Mile Island power station is still in operation, but this sign serves as a reminder of an accident that could easily have been much worse.

Due to a series of errors, one of the plant's four reactors had overheated. This created a huge amount of steam—so much that it caused the reinforced concrete of the reactor to explode. The explosion hurled huge amounts of radioactive material into the air, and caused a fire that lasted for over a week. Fifty-six people were killed in the accident. Radioactive **fallout** spread across Europe and even today, thousands of cases of cancer are blamed on radiation from Chernobyl.

In 2011, a powerful earthquake struck Japan, causing a tsunami. The giant wave hit the Fukushima Nuclear Power Plant and disrupted the cooling systems, which eventually caused three of its reactors to experience meltdown. There was no large explosion, but large amounts of radioactive water were released into the Pacific Ocean.

ГОТЕЛЬ ПОЛІССЯ

Even 30 years after the Chernobyl disaster, the nearby town of Pripyat is still too contaminated for people to live there.

REWIND

Most experts agree that the design of the Chernobyl plant was unsafe and that human error and poor safety procedures caused the disaster. That type of reactor is very rare today and most nuclear power stations follow very strict safety regulations. Do you think Chernobyl played a role in making nuclear safety a priority? Explain your reasons.

A Nuclear World

Many countries use nuclear power, but even more countries do not. Not all countries have the technology or expertise to refine nuclear fuel and build nuclear power stations. Nuclear power is limited to about 30 countries, where it produces around 11 percent of the world's electricity. At the moment, 13 countries depend on nuclear power for at least one quarter of their electricity.

France relies the most on nuclear power. It has more than 50 reactors and uses them to produce almost 75 percent of its energy. In addition, the French company EDF has won contracts to build and operate reactors in other countries. The United States produces almost twice as much nuclear power as France. However, its overall electricity production is much greater than France's, so nuclear energy makes up a smaller portion of the nation's overall total—only about 19 percent.

Changing Trends

The Fukushima disaster caused many countries to rethink their use of nuclear power. It showed how an unavoidable natural disaster could cause a serious accident.

The organizers of Chernobyl tours say that the amount of radiation encountered by the tourists on a short visit is small enough to be safe.

Most countries would like their citizens to have access to clean, cheap electricity. However, they need to balance this against safety and environmental concerns. China, Russia, and India are building more reactors. Others, such as Germany, are reducing their use of nuclear power.

Submarines are hard to track when they are underwater, so being able to stay submerged gives nuclear submarines an advantage.

Other Uses

Some navies use nuclear energy to power submarines and aircraft carriers. Traditional submarines use a mixture of diesel and electrical power. They use batteries when they are under water, but when the batteries run out, they need to come to the surface and use diesel engines to recharge them. A nuclear submarine generates enough electricity to allow it to stay under the water for months at a time.

The Energy Future: You Choose

Some tour operators are now offering tourists the chance to visit Pripyat, near the site of the Chernobyl disaster. There is still radiation present, so many experts say it is too dangerous. Others say that a short visit is not harmful. Would you take the tour? Why would you worry about the future outcome if you did?

The Case Against Nuclear Energy

Even though it has been producing safe, clean energy for many years, nuclear power is still controversial. Many people are against its use and do not want to live near a nuclear power station or a nuclear waste disposal site. Here are some of the main reasons why:

- Health concerns: Scientists still have not come up with a good way of disposing of radioactive waste. The radiation is dangerous, and if it leaked into groundwater or soil, it could cause a health crisis.
- Accidents: Even with improved safety procedures and strict regulations, there is still the risk of a natural disaster such as an earthquake causing a serious accident. Nuclear plants could also be sabotaged by terrorists or other groups.
- Cost: Although they produce electricity cheaply once they are in operation, nuclear power plants are expensive to build.

For decades, some countries stockpiled nuclear weapons to defend themselves from attack. Many people still worry about nuclear attack, especially if the technology spreads to more countries and groups.

- Water: The cooling systems in a nuclear reactor use a lot of water. In many places, water is an important resource that must be conserved.
- Weapons: The fuel and processes used in nuclear plants could also be used to make deadly nuclear weapons. Some people worry that the widespread use of nuclear technology makes it more likely that terrorist groups, or extremists groups or countries, will get their hands on nuclear weapons.
- Decommissioning: Nuclear power stations eventually become outdated and need to be **decommissioned**, or shut down. Making the land safe again can be a long and expensive process.

These campaigners are protesting against the building of new nuclear reactors.

The Energy Future: You Choose

Many of the arguments against nuclear power have to do with the risk of disasters. However, accidents can happen at many other types of power plants, too. The vast majority of nuclear reactors run safely and efficiently. Is the relatively small risk of disaster worth eliminating such an efficient source of power? Give reasons for your answers and support them with examples from this book and other resources.

The Case for Nuclear Energy

In spite of the potential problems with nuclear energy, there are still a lot of good reasons for using it. Here are just a few of them:

- Greenhouse gases: Nuclear power plants produce very small amounts of greenhouse gases, such as carbon dioxide. This means that they do not really contribute to climate change, which gives them an advantage over coal-fired or gas-fired power stations.
- Cost: Once they are built, nuclear power stations are cheap to operate. A nuclear power station can provide electricity for a city of 1 million people by reacting less than 7 pounds (3 kg) of fuel a day.
- Stable power: Unlike wind and solar power, which depend on the weather and do not provide a constant supply of power, nuclear power stations are not dependent on external factors and can produce electricity almost constantly. Some types of reactors can even be refueled without having to be shut down.

Melting sea ice caused by climate change causes problems for penguins. Using nuclear power is one way to reduce greenhouse gas emissions and halt climate change.

- Location: Geothermal or solar power can be used only where the conditions are right, such as in sunny climates or places where there are hot rocks not too deep underground. Nuclear power stations can be built in a much wider range of locations.

- Sustainability: Compared to the amount of coal used in coal-fired power stations, nuclear power stations use relatively small amounts of fuel, so uranium supplies will last a long time. New types of reactors may be able to use even less fuel or produce fuel themselves.

One of the main downsides of wind and solar power is that they work only when the wind is blowing or the sun is shining.

The Energy Future: You Choose

Now that you know the pros and cons of nuclear energy, it is up to you to decide which issues are the most important. Weigh the good points of nuclear energy against the bad points. Do you think that it is a good way to meet our energy needs? If the answer is yes, would you feel differently if a nuclear power station were being built near your home? Give reasons for your answers and provide examples from this book and other further reading.

The Future Is... Fusion?

Scientists hope that in the not-too-distant future, we may be able to generate electricity by using a different type of nuclear reaction: fusion. In nuclear fission, atoms are split apart. In nuclear fusion, they are fused, or joined, to create new substances. This process releases energy. It is the same reaction that happens inside the Sun, generating heat and light.

Inside the Sun, two atoms of hydrogen (with one proton each) join together to form a helium atom with two protons. The process releases neutrons, as well as huge amounts of energy. In the Sun, this process is possible because of the extremely high temperatures and the immense pressure found there. It is very difficult to replicate these conditions on Earth. We can use microwaves and lasers to achieve the temperatures, and **electromagnets** to create pressure. However, doing this uses huge amounts of energy—more than the reaction is able to produce.

Achieving fusion means creating the nuclear reactions that take place in the Sun.

First Steps

Some countries have already used fusion in nuclear weapons. Although the first nuclear bombs used fission, fusion bombs were soon developed. They are much more powerful than fission bombs. However, generating energy from fusion requires a stable, long-lasting reaction. The technology of fusion bombs does not allow that.

Scientists in many countries are working hard on fusion. In 2013, researchers in the United States were able to generate more energy than that used by their experiment, but only by a tiny amount. Still, it is an important step in the quest for efficient fusion.

The Alcator C-Mod fusion experiment at Massachusetts Institute of Technology (MIT) uses a type of device called a tokamak.

FAST FORWARD

If scientists are able to achieve fusion, it could completely change the world. It would provide cheap and plentiful energy with very little pollution. If this happened, what do you think would happen to the **economies** of countries that produce other types of fuel, such as oil and gas? Explain your thinking.

Power Up!

Nuclear energy has the potential to help the planet. Nuclear power stations release hardly any greenhouse gases, so nuclear energy is a much better option for producing electricity than coal, oil, or natural gas. We could cut down on greenhouse gases even more if we used electric cars instead of cars that use gas. Electric cars, can be recharged using electricity from a nuclear power station. However, we still need to develop a safe way of disposing of nuclear waste.

What Can You Do?

You can help reduce greenhouse gases in your daily life. Try to cut down on the amount of electricity you use in your home by turning off lights, appliances, and gadgets when not in use. Walk, ride a bicycle, or take a bus instead of using a car.

Teaching kids today about using power sparingly could create a better future for the next generations.

Activity

Nuclear fission is a tricky concept that took scientists many years to figure out and master. Here is a simple activity that will help you visualize what takes place during nuclear fission.

You Will Need:

- A long, skinny balloon (the type used for making balloon animals)
- A pair of scissors
- A partner

Instructions

1. Blow up the balloon but leave a little room so that you can twist it in half. Tie off the end. This represents the nucleus of an atom of nuclear fuel, such as U-235.
2. Twist the balloon in the center to create two separate sections of equal size.
3. Use both hands to pinch the balloon tightly on each side of the twist.
4. Ask your partner to use the scissors to cut the twisted portion of the balloon. This represents a neutron smashing into the nucleus and causing it to split in two.
5. Hold tightly onto the ends of the two smaller balloons, then release them and let them fly off. The energy of their movement represents the energy released by the reaction.
6. Collect the balloon fragments—these make up your "nuclear waste." Think about how you can dispose of them safely.

What Happened?

In a real fission reaction, each splitting nucleus releases neutrons as well as energy. The neutrons then smash into other atoms, releasing more energy and even more loose neutrons. This causes a chain reaction, which could continue until all the fuel is used up. In a nuclear reactor, other substances are used to control the speed of the reaction.

Glossary

Please note: Some bold-faced words are defined where they appear in the text

atoms The smallest possible parts of an element

climate change The increase in the temperature of the atmosphere near Earth's surface that can contribute to changes in global climate patterns

coolant A liquid, often water, that is used to keep machines cool

economies The systems by which goods and services are produced, sold, and bought

electromagnets Type of magnets in which the magnetic field is produced by an electric current

electrons Tiny particles with a negative charge that move outside the nucleus of an atom

enriched Purified and made more concentrated

environment The conditions of the area where you live

fallout The radioactive particles that are produced by a nuclear explosion and that fall through the atmosphere

fossil fuels Energy sources made from the remains of plants and animals that died millions of years ago and were buried

generator A machine that changes motion into electrical energy

greenhouse gases Gases in the atmosphere that contribute to the greenhouse effect

isotopes Different forms of the same element

megawatts (MW) Units of measure for energy; There are 1 million watts in a megawatt.

meltdown An accident in a nuclear reactor in which the fuel overheats and melts the reactor core

moderator A substance that slows down neutrons in nuclear fission

nuclear fission A chemical process in which the nucleus of an atom is split into smaller parts, releasing energy at the same time

nuclear fusion A chemical process in which the nuclei of two or more atoms fuse into a more massive nucleus, releasing a huge amount of energy

nuclear reactions Processes in which the structure of an atomic nucleus is changed

nucleus The center of something, such as an atom

neutrons A particle in the nucleus of an atom

pressure The force that is produced when something presses or pushes against other things

protons A positively-charged particle in the nucleus of an atom

radiation Waves of energy sent out by sources of heat or light, such as the Sun or by radioactive substances

radioactive Giving off high-energy rays and particles

reactors The structures in which nuclear reactions can take place

turbines Machines with rotating blades

uranium A dense gray metal that can be used as nuclear fuel

Learning More

Find out more about alternative energy and nuclear power.

Books

Mclean, Adam. *What is Atomic Theory?* (Shaping Modern Science). Crabtree Publishing, 2011.

Oxlade, Chris. *Nuclear Energy* (Tales of Invention). Heinemann-Raintree, 2011.

Owen, Ruth. *Energy From Atoms: Nuclear Power* (Power: Yesterday, Today, Tomorrow). PowerKids Press, 2013.

Reynoldson, Fiona. *Understanding Nuclear Power* (The World of Energy).Gareth Stevens Publishing, 2010.

Spilsbury, Richard and Louise. *Nuclear Power* (Let's Discuss Energy Resources). PowerKids Press, 2011.

Websites

This website features facts about nuclear energy, as well as a map showing the nuclear reactors in the United States:
www.fplsafetyworld.com/?ver=kkblue&utilid=fplforkids&id=16182

Visit this site to learn about careers in nuclear engineering:
www.nuclearconnect.org/in-the-classroom/for-students/careers

This government site has plenty of facts and statistics about energy usage in the US:
www.eia.gov/kids/energy.cfm?page=nuclear_home-basics

Index